Endorsements

This simple but masterfully created angel book will appeal to both angel novice and scholar alike. Combined with a search into the Word of God on these powerful warriors place in a believer's life, anyone can discover what real value the Father has invested in each of His children's gifting and destiny!

Author -Debra Smith Joy, Creator of Friends of Kat Kerr FB Group

Seeing Angels in the Sky
Photos by Robin Bremer
Interview of Kat Kerr

Copyright 2016

About Angels

Angels are everywhere, working the plans of God out in our lives. I have been a Christian for almost 35 years but was always taught to be fearful of angels least I am worshiping them. I have always been drawn to the sky at night and in the day time since a child, laying out on a hill looking up at the sky. I gave my life to God at 13 years of age.

Several years ago my life was changed when I started to listen to Kat Kerr, a women who God has mandated to take to heaven and then has her teach and share what He shows her. She has inspired me to ask my Daddy to open my eyes to see the "Host of Heaven" which is what they like to be called, hiding in the clouds spying on the enemy and protection the children of God. From her I have learned the authority I have "in Christ" and how to send my angels out to do God's words that I speak.

This book is a record of God's love, humor and creativity and evidence of His supernatural weapons He has given us to bring Heaven on earth. My hope is that you too will become as a child as you search for the host hidden in each picture and will jump and shout with joy as your eyes see the host. I pray that you ask Daddy to open your eyes to see the Host all around you in every day life and that you learn how to send them on missions and treasure hunts.

There are pictures on the side of every photo that shows a yellow outline of the angels face. I did this so you could easily see the pictures of the host. Every quote of Kat Kerr under the pictures are noted with "KK" to show that this was her answer to a question. Notice that through out this book angels are referred to as angels or host.

In the back of the book I have links to other books on Angels and Command Prayer.

If you have never made Jesus the Lord of your life and would like to please say this simple prayer. "Jesus be the Lord of my life" today the angels party because you just became part of the family!

Beautiful wolf or puppy face!

EVERY person has an angel sent at conception to protect and minister to them.

Large pig type Host face.

The angels were created in tribes just like on earth. Earth is a copy of Heaven. Michele and his angles are the warrior angels. They are strange and fierce looking. They are not "Pretty Boys".

If you ask God to open your eyes so you can see the angels or "Host of Heaven" as they like to be called you will begin to see them in the sky. This picture is of a rabbit looking host and this is the first time I saw him.

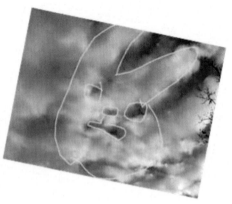

I find that if you step away from these pictures and look at them from a greater distance you can see the host of Heaven better. This is the same rabbit looking host I saw in an earlier picture.

When you look in the sky to see the host, look for odd shapes and patterns. Often time the thing I will see most and first are the **eyes.** When you look at the pictures you will find MORE faces than just the ones I have circled. It is like looking at a supernatural puzzle and it's additive!

Perfect Nose!

There are many angels hiding is the clouds in the sky ministering to the saints and recording what the enemy is doing.

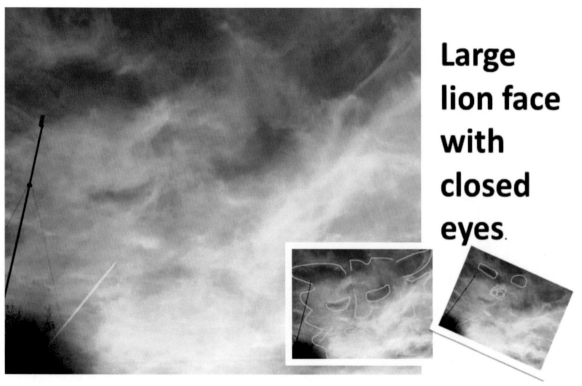

Large lion face with closed eyes.

You can direct the host of heaven by speaking Gods word and telling them to go and do it.

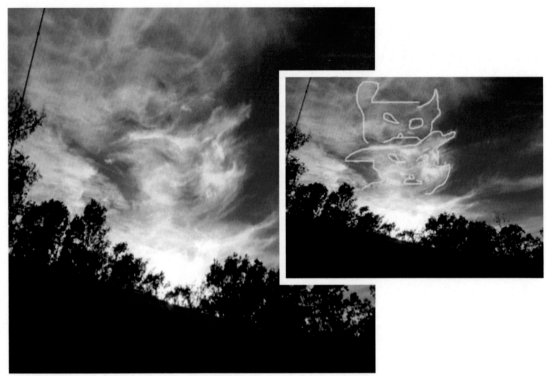

If you take pictures of strange shapes in the sky you will begin to train your eyes to see the angels. When you take a picture of the host and look at it in your camera you will be able to "see" them better because the camera makes the picture much smaller and detailed.

Your angels are there to minister to YOU, don't let them get bored by never sending them out to do things. Michael's warrior tribe are strong and strange looking. Some of them are built like weapons and are transformers!

**Beautiful
lion
blowing.**

Our angels get very excited when we make the right choices and do everything within the power God gives them to protect us.-KK

Following are the answers to question I asked Kat Kerr in an interview. The Lord has taken Kat to heaven many times and asked her to record what she saw. When asked how many types of angels are there? There are millions of Angels and too many types to mention as God is unlimited in His creativity.-KK

The Dancer
with a veil.

Does our guardian angel have feelings of love or compassion for the person they are assigned to? Yes, they are assigned to us at the time of conception and remain with us all our lives. -KK

What is the smallest, largest, and strangest angel you have seen and what do they do? The smallest ones I have seen are those who care for the flowers in Heaven. -KK

Aragon

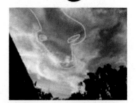

The largest angel you have ever seen? One of the Host of Heaven (a Fire angel who serves in the armies of Heaven) and he was 200 feet tall bring a deposit of the Fire from Heaven into our city. -KK

Your guardian angel has a special affection for you that comes from the Father, and sometimes even likes the same food or things we like here on earth. -KK

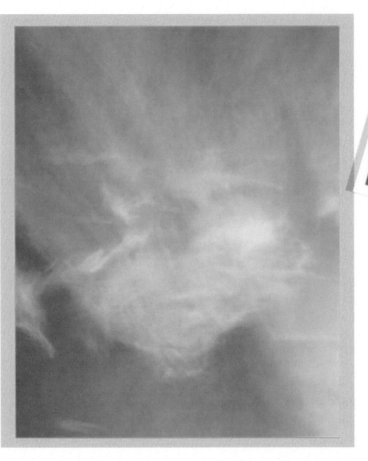

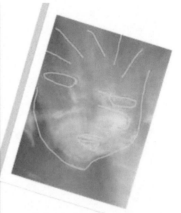

What do angels do when the person they are assigned to dies? They return to Heaven for a much needed restoration, probably not very happy that the person they have guarded all their life was just dragged to Hell and they could do nothing to stop it!-KK

Do angels have a sense of humor? Angels have many of the same feelings as we do and humor is definitely one of them.-KK

What are some of the things you have seen angels do working on earth? I have seen Scribe angels recording our words and courier angels collecting worship.

I have also seen messenger angels deliver the replacement body parts. Usually most of the angels I see are the warring angels fighting the demons.-KK

The largest angels I saw were the 200 foot Fire Angels, made out of light and smoke and the strangest ones were just big eyeballs with wings. The Father sends them around the earth, recording our lives. -KK

Does every person born have an guardian angel? Yes.-KK

Aragon blowing fire.

If a baby has been aborted or lost what do they do? They carry their own assigned child, home to Heaven.-KK

Fiery Mane

What do you think the scripture means when it says we will not be given in marriage or marrying in heaven but we will be like the angels? The angels never marry, nor are they given to be married, which is exactly how Believers are that go to Heaven.-KK

What kind of work do the angels do in heaven? They care for millions of babies in the nurseries and also help to keep everything in order.-KK

Host eyes!

What makes angels sad? When we disobey God and when we are mean to each other.-KK

Some angels are small, delicate and some look like little children so they can become the play partners of little children who come to HEAVEN.-KK

Our angels even help escort us home to Heaven when we die.-KK

Beautiful giant eye.

Do angels appear from different nationalities? Yes, I have seen many types of Angels.-KK

Do our prayers affect the angels? Absolutely.-KK

Can angels change the way they appear to us? Yes, especially in line with their current assignment.-KK

A Host looking in my window.

What happens to angels when we worship? They love it and start singing too!! -KK

Host looking in my window another time.

What do angels do when we dance in worship? They usually start dancing first-KK.

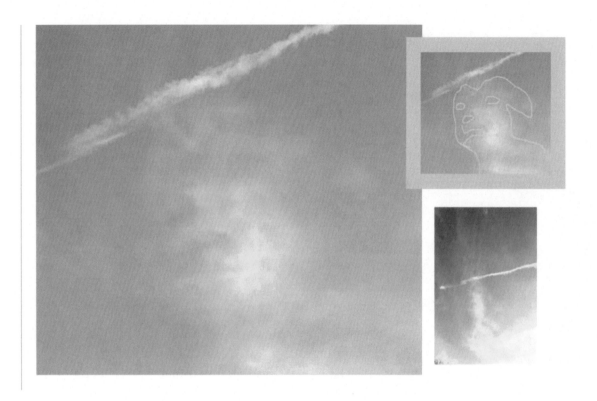

How can we tell that Angels are near? Most people can 'feel' their presence.-KK

Do our angels look like us? Not all of them-KK.

About the Author

Robin Bremer is an ordained minister, who has appeared several times on the National TV show "With God You Will Succeed" and "The Deborah Sweetin Show". She has also been a guest on national and local radio shows. She is the author of over 37 books for adults and children. Her calling is to bring God's presence and Supernatural Power through the message of the KINGDOM of JOY and to set people free from a godless religion of "doing and works" into a personal, SUPERNATURAL relationship with Jesus Christ. Follow Robins' blog http://www.robinbremer.net RobinBremer@sbcglobal.net. Follow Robin on her Author Central page at: http://amazon.com/author/robinbremer

Look for more in this series coming soon!

MORE on ANGELS

Commanding Angels... Where does it say We can do that?

https://www.youtube.com/watch?v=top2OGts9ZU

How to Command Your Angels

https://www.youtube.com/watch?v=NDQn6JQcuC8

Angels and Your Imagination

https://www.youtube.com/watch?v=dCgTsjhBPPc

About Kat Kerr

Author / Speaker, Kat Kerr will challenge what you have believed about Heaven, the "other" dimension (spirit realm), this life, death and even eternity. Since 1996 she has been 'caught up' by the Spirit of God and taken on amazing journeys into the Third Heaven as well as to Hell. She lives and moves in the supernatural which gives her a detailed understanding of how God, His angels and even darkness operate today. You will feel the manifest presence of God as she shares what it is like to stand before the living God in the Throne Room. The Father has given hard evidence in her Revealing Heaven series that proves Heaven truly exists and that you will live a literal life there.

http://www.katkerr.com/

https://www.revealingheaven.com/

https://www.youtube.com/user/TheKatKerr

https://www.facebook.com/TheRevelatorKatKerr/

More Angel Information:

https://www.amazon.com/Angels-Facts-Answers-Robin-Bremer-ebook/dp/B00E8VC1KY

https://www.amazon.com/Raising-Angels-Supernatural-Christian-Experience/dp/1499631251

https://www.amazon.com/Dont-Just-Sit-There-Do-Something-ebook/dp/B01MXCW21B

Bible Study Courses

For the full Bible Course-

Spirit, Soul & Body Deliverance Bible Study Course go to:

http://robinbremer.net/digital-store/

Supernatural Bible Study Course

3 Teacher's Guides
3 Book
9 MP3'S Classes
9 MP4'S Classes

1 Bonus book "Raising The Dead, Angels, Supernatural Wine & Other Normal Christian Experiences"

Best-Selling Author Robin Bremer

That's a lot of stuff!

More Books By Robin

http://amazon.com/author/robinbremer
2016
Finding Your Identity in the Armor
Word Seeds
You Are a Spirit, You Live in a Body, & You Have a Soul
All Things Are Yours
Kingdom Living Series Vo. 1-3
- The Joy of Kingdom Driven Living
- Kingdom Justice & Liberty for All
- Pursuing the Kingdom Mandate

Kingdom Living Bible Study Course Vol. 1-3
- Change Me Lord
- Take Me Deeper Lord
- Use Me Lord

Pocket Study Guides Vol.1
- Kingdom Confessions

The Kingdom Joy Series
- Supernatural Witnessing Made Easy
- Joy The Wine of Heaven

- Taking Authority, Dominion & Subdue
- Taking Healing: Your Legal Right to Health & Healing
- Hindrances To Receiving Your Healing

80 Facts & Answers about Angels
Use Your Words
42 Hints for a Fun & Successful Convention
How to Have Peace Anywhere Anytime
Prayer, Partnering With the Holy Spirit
Children's Books
Ribbons the Clown Coloring Book
Praise Party
Kids' Prayer Power
Audio Books
The Joy of Kingdom Driven Living
Raising the Dead and Other Normal Christian
Kingdom Confessions

Follow Robin on Her Social Media

http://facebook.com/feedmypeoplejoy

https://www.facebook.com/RobinBremerAuthorCoach/

http://www.youtube.com/user/feedmypeoplejoy

http://www.twitter.com/feedmypeoplejoy

http://pinterest.com/robinbremer

www.linkedin.com/pub/rev-robin-bremer/42/397/b7a/

http://robinbremer.net/digital-store/

Made in the USA
San Bernardino, CA
07 January 2017